My Coloring Book
(BIRDS)

DO AMAZING THINGS

Flamingo Color by Number

Use the key at the bottom of the page to color the picture.

1. pink   2. blue   3. green
4. gray   5. brown   6. black

Name: _____   Date: _____

Birds A to Z

Color the bird and trace the word

American Robin

Name: _____   Date: _____

Birds A to Z

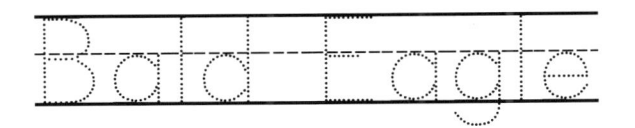

Color the bird and trace the word

Bald Eagle

Name: Date:

Birds A to Z

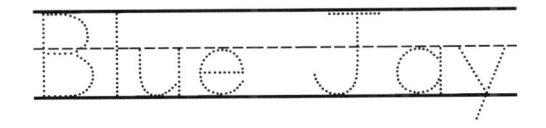

Color the bird and trace the word

Blue Jay

Name: _____ Date: _____

Birds A to Z

Color the bird and trace the word

Northern Cardinal

Name: _____ Date: _____

Birds A to Z

Color the bird and trace the word

European Starling

Name: _____ Date: _____

Birds A to Z

Color the bird and trace the word

House Sparrow

Name: _____ Date: _____

Birds A to Z

Color the bird and trace the word

Mourning Dove

Name: _____   Date: _____

Birds A to Z

Color the bird and trace the word

American

Goldfinch

Name: _____ Date: _____

Birds A to Z

Color the bird and trace the word

Australian Magpie

Name: _____ Date: _____

Birds A to Z

Color the bird and trace the word

Cinnamon Teal

Name: _____ Date: _____

Birds A to Z

Color the bird and trace the word

Magnificent

Frigatebird

Name: _____   Date: _____

Birds A to Z

Color the bird and trace the word

Stork

Name: _____ Date: _____

Birds A to Z

Color the bird and trace the word

Guianan

Name: _____ Date: _____

Birds A to Z

Color the bird and trace the word

Atlantic Canary

Name: Date:

Birds A to Z

Color the bird and trace the word

Snowy Plover

Name: _____   Date: _____

Birds A to Z

Color the bird and trace the word

Nicobar Pigeon

Name: _____ Date: _____

Birds A to Z

Color the bird and trace the word

RedNuthatch

Name: _____   Date: _____

Birds A to Z

Color the bird and trace the word

Albatross

THINK Positive

Made in the USA
Columbia, SC
17 May 2023